RICK MIDDLETON

EDDIE SHORE

TERRY O'REILLY

JOE THORNTON

NORMAN GAINOR

JOHN BUCYK

BOBBY ORR

RAY BOURQUE

CAM NEELY

PHIL ESPOSITO

SERGEI SAMSONOV

FRANKIE BRIMSEK

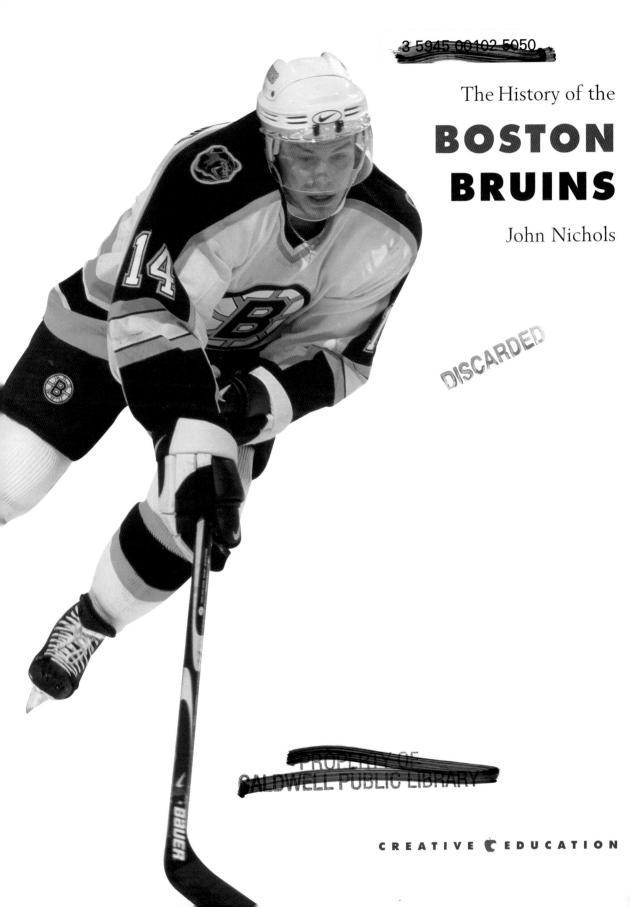

The History of the

BOSTON
BRUINS

John Nichols

CREATIVE ⦿ EDUCATION

Published by Creative Education, 123 South Broad Street, Mankato, MN 56001

Creative Education is an imprint of The Creative Company.

Designed by Rita Marshall.

Photographs by Getty Images (Steve Babineau/Allsport), Hockey Hall of Fame (Graphic Artists,

London Life-Portnoy), Icon Sports Media Inc. (Robert Beck), Reuters, Sports Gallery Inc.

(Al Messerschmidt), SportsChrome USA (Gregg Forwerck)

Library of Congress Cataloging-in-Publication Data

Nichols, John, 1966– The history of the Boston Bruins / by John Nichols.

p. cm. — (Stanley Cup champions)   ISBN 1-58341-275-1

Summary: A history of the winning Boston hockey team from its first

season in 1924 to the present.

1. Boston Bruins (Hockey team)—History—Juvenile literature.

[1. Boston Bruins (Hockey team)—History.] I. Title. II. Series.

GV848.B6 N53 2003   796.962'64'0974461—dc21   2002034762

First Edition 9 8 7 6 5 4 3 2 1

THE CITY OF BOSTON IS THE CAPITAL OF MASSACHUSETTS.

LOCATED IN AMERICA'S NEW ENGLAND REGION,

BOSTON IS A BUSTLING HARBOR TOWN WITH A RICH

history that dates back to the days of the American Revolution. It

was here that Paul Revere made his famous midnight ride, and

modern Boston is home to many of the nation's oldest and finest

educational, financial, cultural, and medical centers.

Boston is also famous for its love of sports. Perhaps the team

nearest the hearts of Boston sports fans is the National Hockey

League's (NHL) Boston Bruins. Founded in 1924, the franchise drew

its name from a contest in which entries were to relate to an

untamed animal of "size, strength, agility, ferocity, and cunning." The

Bruins—another word for bears—have been prowling the ranks of

the NHL ever since.

ART ROSS

{THE BABY BRUINS} In the 1920s, the NHL consisted of only six teams: the Boston Bruins, Chicago Blackhawks, Detroit Red Wings, New York Rangers, Montreal Canadiens, and Toronto Maple Leafs. The first edition of the Bruins won only six of 30 games in 1924–25. But what the Bruins lacked in talent, they made up for in leadership. Head coach and general manager Art Ross quickly established himself as one of the finest minds in the game. Over the next 30 years, Ross molded the Bruins franchise into a tough and fiercely competitive winner. Ross's impact on the game was so great that the NHL named its award for the league's leading scorer after him—the Art Ross Trophy.

The first-year Bruins took their lumps, losing one game 1–10 (the worst defeat in club history).

One of Ross's best early moves was signing a bruising young defenseman by the name of Eddie Shore. The 5-foot-11 and 190-pound Shore debuted in 1926 and immediately improved Boston's

KEN BELANGER

Aubrey "Dit" Clapper spent 20 seasons in Boston and made the Hall of Fame.

AUBREY CLAPPER

fortunes. Shore's swift skating, uncanny playmaking, and fearsome

hitting made him the Bruins' first true star. "Shore plays like some-

one on the other team stole something from him," said

Bruins wing Harry Oliver. "He leaves bruises."

As the 1920s wore on, Boston continued to

improve. Along with Shore, the Bruins featured such

standouts as center Ralph "Cooney" Weiland and

wingers Norman "Dutch" Gainor and Aubrey "Dit" Clapper.

Together, Weiland, Gainor, and Clapper formed a goal-scoring unit

so explosive that it became known as the "Dynamite Line."

Led by Shore and the Dynamite Line, the 1928–29 Bruins cap-

tured the American Division title. In the playoffs, Boston stormed

past the Montreal Canadiens and the New York Rangers to capture

the NHL championship and the Stanley Cup—the silver chalice

that is hockey's most valued prize.

In **1929–30**, star Cecil Thompson won the first of four Vezina Trophies as hockey's top goalie.

CECIL THOMPSON

Like Eddie Shore, Don Sweeney was a longtime defensive standout for the Bruins.

DON SWEENEY

Boston remained a strong team throughout the 1930s but struggled in the playoffs. Between 1930 and 1938, Boston made

The talented Bruins squad of **1940–41** went 23 games in a row without a loss—a team record.

seven trips to the postseason and was knocked out every time, despite a potent offense that featured forwards Milt Schmidt, Woody Dumart, and Bobby Bauer.

Finally, in 1939, the Bruins ended their playoff frustration by defeating the Toronto Maple Leafs and capturing the Stanley Cup for the second time. The unexpected star of that season was rookie goalie Frankie Brimsek. His 10 shutouts and 1.58 goals-against average were good enough to earn him the Calder Trophy as the league's Rookie of the Year and the Vezina Trophy as the NHL's top goalie. Brimsek was so dominant that his teammates nicknamed him "Mr. Zero."

{FROM SHORE TO BUCYK} During the 1939–40 season, an era of Bruins hockey came to an end with the trade of Eddie Shore

WOODY DUMART

to the New York Americans. But even without its former star,

Boston put together an impressive 27–8–13 record in 1940–41. Led

by Clapper, the Bruins defeated Toronto in the playoffs to earn

another trip to the finals. Boston then swept the Detroit Red Wings

in four straight games to claim its third Stanley Cup.

For the next 19 seasons, Boston remained a contender and made the Stanley Cup Finals in 1946, 1953, 1957, and 1958. High-scoring

players such as center Fleming Mackell kept the Bruins in the hunt for

In a stunning offensive display, Leo LaBine netted five goals in a single period in a **1954** game.

the Cup. But each time Boston made the finals, it was

turned away by the Montreal Canadiens. "We had some

mighty fine clubs during the '50s," said hard-charging

wing Leo LaBine. "But no matter how good we were,

Montreal was always just a little bit better."

As the 1950s ended, so did Boston's long stretch of winning

hockey. From 1960 to 1967, the Bruins posted losing records and

missed the playoffs each year. But even during this dismal stretch,

Bruins fans had reasons to cheer.

One of those reasons was named John Bucyk. Bucyk played

right wing and wore the number 9 Boston sweater from 1958 to

1978. The rugged 6-foot-1 and 190-pounder scored 545 goals

during his career (the most in Bruins history) and kept hope alive

JOHN BUCYK

during the dark times. "John worked harder and gave more to this organization than anybody will ever know," said wing Ken Hodge, a longtime teammate. "John *is* Boston Bruins hockey."

{ORR AND ESPO' LEAD THE WAY} Boston's losing ways ended when the team signed an 18-year-old defenseman by the name of Bobby Orr. The intelligent, broad-shouldered youngster came into the league heralded as the NHL's next big star, and his dazzling combination of speed, stick-handling, and creativity redefined modern hockey.

Before Orr came along, defensemen rarely ventured far from their own net and contributed little offensively. But Orr's blazing speed and great agility allowed him to venture deep into enemy territory and create scoring chances. In 1966–67, Orr scored 41 points (goals plus assists) in 61 games and won the Calder Trophy. "Many times I saw Bobby carry the puck from behind his own net, weave through about three or four guys, get a hard shot on goal, and then—BOOM—he'd beat the other team back down the ice before they could get a rush going," said Bruins wing Wayne Cashman.

As the 1960s wore on, the Bruins built a winner around their boy-wonder defenseman and the veteran Bucyk. Stars such as

Defenseman Bobby Orr often joined the Bruins' offensive attack, scoring 264 career goals.

BOBBY ORR

Phil Esposito reigned as Boston's top scorer every season from **1967–68** to **1974–75**.

Hodge and high-scoring center Phil Esposito were acquired in a

trade. Cashman and Don Marcotte provided scoring punch from the

wings, Gerry Cheevers developed into a top goal-

tender, and flashy center Derek Sanderson followed

Orr as the Calder Trophy winner in 1968.

This collection of hard-charging young stars pro-

pelled the Bruins back into championship contention.

In 1969–70, behind Orr's 120 points and Esposito's 43 goals, Boston

romped through the regular season. In the playoffs, the Bruins

quickly dispatched New York and Chicago to set up a Stanley Cup

Finals showdown with the St. Louis Blues.

Boston easily won the first three games of the series, but in

game four, St. Louis held a 3–2 lead in the third period. With time

running out, Bucyk netted the tying goal, sending the game into

sudden-death overtime. Early in overtime, Orr joined a Boston rush.

GERRY CHEEVERS

Zipping past a defender, the fleet defenseman streaked toward the

St. Louis goal and snapped a perfect Sanderson pass into the net.

Feet taken out by a Blues defender's stick, and arms outstretched in

victory, Orr appeared to fly as he clinched the championship.

Orr and Esposito led the way again in 1971–72 as the "Big Bad

Bruins" posted a 54–13–11 record. Boston's dominance continued in the postseason as the Bruins rolled past Toronto, St. Louis, and New York on their way to a fifth Stanley Cup championship.

{BLUE-COLLAR BRUINS} Boston continued to ride the strong shoulders of Orr and Esposito until the 1975–76 season, when crippling knee injuries sidelined Orr, and Esposito was traded to New York for defenseman Brad Park and center Jean Ratelle. Orr would never be the same, sitting out a season and then retiring after a brief comeback with the Chicago Blackhawks. Between them, Orr and Esposito captured the Hart Trophy (as the league's Most Valuable Player) five times and the Ross Trophy (as the league's leading scorer) seven times during their reign in Boston.

Without their two marquee stars, the Bruins found a different way to win. Fiery new coach Don Cherry preached a blue-collar style that emphasized hustle, body checking, and hard work. "My

BRAD PARK

Star wing Rick Middleton averaged 45 goals a season from **1978–79** to **1983–84**.

RICK MIDDLETON

guys don't skate that well and aren't real nifty with the puck," said

Cherry, "but they bring their lunchpail to work every night and spill

their guts on that ice."

The inspirational leader of the new Bruins was

Terry O'Reilly. The 6-foot-1 and 200-pound wing was

an immediate favorite of Boston's large Irish popula-

tion, and his scrappy, brawling style often overshad-

During his Bruins career, Terry O'Reilly spent a whopping 2,095 minutes in the penalty box.

owed his solid goal-scoring skills. O'Reilly and defenseman Mike

Milbury provided the grit for the Bruins' success in the late 1970s,

while Park, Ratelle, and winger Rick Middleton provided the polish.

The Bruins reached the Stanley Cup Finals twice during

Cherry's tenure as head coach, losing in 1977 and 1978 to their

longtime nemesis, the Montreal Canadiens. Cherry left the team in

1979 for a career in broadcasting. As the hot-blooded coach left the

stage, another Bruins great was about to enter.

TERRY O'REILLY

{A RAY OF LIGHT} Boston's long history of great defensemen

continued when the team drafted Ray Bourque with the top overall

pick in the 1979 NHL Draft. Like Shore and Orr before him,

Bourque made an immediate impact, scoring 65 points in 1979–80

and winning the Calder Trophy.

Also like his famous predecessors, Bourque possessed uncommon offensive skills while sacrificing nothing on defense. His speed, strength, and uncommonly hard shot complemented a deep understanding of the game. "You never catch Ray out of position," noted Bruins goalie Andy Moog. "He anticipates everything so well, it's almost like he knows what you are going to do before you do."

Along with his many talents, Bourque was also iron-man consistent. He played 21 seasons in Boston and made the All-Star team 18 times. During his career, he played alongside Bruins stars Terry O'Reilly in the '70s, center Barry Pederson in the '80s, wing Cam Neely in the '90s, and center Joe Thornton at the dawn of the 21st century. While all left their mark on Bruins history, Bourque was the tie that bound them together.

The pinnacle of the Bourque era came during the late 1980s and early '90s, when Bourque and the high-scoring Neely spurred

The great Ray Bourque won the James Norris Trophy (as the game's top defender) five times.

RAY BOURQUE

the Bruins to the Stanley Cup Finals twice. In 1988, the Bruins beat

Buffalo, Montreal, and New Jersey en route to a finals matchup

with the Wayne Gretzky-led Edmonton Oilers. The

Bruins played their hearts out but were swept by the

Oilers in four straight games. Boston returned to the

finals in 1990 but was turned away again by the

mighty Oilers in five games.

Boston remained a strong team throughout the mid-1990s, but

as the decade drew to a close, so did the Bruins' remarkable run of

winning hockey. Injuries, free agency, and age slowed the team. In

1996–97, Boston suffered a losing season for the first time in 30 years.

{BRINGING BACK THE GROWL} In the 1997 NHL Draft,

Boston used the first overall pick to select Joe Thornton, a 6-foot-4

and 210-pound center from London, Ontario. Despite his boyish

grin and mop of blond hair, the young center was a bruiser who

CAM NEELY

enjoyed delivering thunderous body checks nearly as much as scoring goals. Thornton's first two seasons with the Bruins were humbling, as he played against grown men for the first time in his life. Fortunately for the Bruins, another rookie—winger Sergei Samsonov—broke through in 1997–98 with 47 points, a feat that earned him the Calder Trophy.

After being named team captain, Jason Allison doled out a career-high 59 assists in **2000–01**.

Led by Samsonov, Bourque, center Jason Allison, and goaltender Byron Dafoe, the Bruins were a solid team but were not championship-caliber. Looking to the future, the team traded Bourque to the Colorado Avalanche late in the 1999–00 season for some younger talent. Fortunately for Bruins fans, as Bourque departed, Thornton emerged as a star. The big center scored 23 goals in 1999–00 and 37 goals in 2000–01. "Joe is a man now," said defenseman Don Sweeney. "He knows this team needs him to step

JASON ALLISON

Young Russian wing Sergei Samsonov added speed to the Bruins' offensive attack.

SERGEI SAMSONOV

A powerful force at both ends of the ice, Joe Thornton was a Boston star on the rise.

JOE THORNTON

up and be the leader. It's his show now."

In 2001–02, Thornton and the Bruins took a major step for-

ward. Sparked by a trade that sent Jason Allison to the Los Angeles Kings for center Jozef Stumpel and high-scoring wing Glen Murray, the Bruins went 43–24–6 to capture the Northeast Division title. Although Boston's season ended with a first-round playoff loss to the Montreal Canadiens, the Bruins were growling again.

The Boston Bruins have a history of excellence that dates back to the birth of the NHL. Over the years, the franchise has consistently produced some of the game's brightest stars and most exciting moments. Boasting five Stanley Cups and a history of hockey greats, the Bruins and their fans are looking forward to a future as brilliant as their past.

NICK BOYNTON